I0749474

# PSYCHOPATHOLOGY:

# COGNITIOM, EMOTION, AND MOTIVATION

# Table of Contents

## Psychopathology

The exploration of psychopathology involves the analysis of mental illnesses and atypical behaviors, aiming to comprehend their origins, symptoms, and interventions. To develop a thorough grasp of the topic, it is essential to consider the range of elements that can determine the emergence of psychopathology. Cognition, emotion, in addition motivation are significant effects that can have a key influence on the emergence and expression of psychopathology. Within psychopathology, cognition, emotion, and motivation can refer to abnormal psychological processes in these areas. This can manifest in various mental disorders such as schizophrenia, depression, and anxiety disorders, where individuals may experience distorted thinking patterns, intense emotional disturbances, and disruptions in motivation (Kube et al., 2020). These abnormalities can greatly impact an individual's perception of reality, capacity to control their emotions, and drive to engage in goal-directed behaviors.

Cognition encompasses the mental activities of acquiring information and comprehension, including thinking, remembering, understanding, making decisions, and solving problems. In psychopathology, distorted cognitive patterns and dysfunctional thinking are significant factors. Theories on depression propose that negative automatic thoughts, overgeneralization, and catastrophizing (assuming the worst possible outcome conclusion) influence the manifestation and persistence of depressive conditions (Jiang, 2024). Additionally, individuals with psychopathology may have distorted or unhealthy thought patterns that influence their symptoms (Kube et al., 2020). Those experiencing depression could have a bias towards negative interpretations of neutral situations, which can worsen their symptoms (Kube et al., 2020). Also, individuals with disorders like schizophrenia may experience disruptions in cognitive functions like attention, memory, and executive functioning. This highlights the importance of cognition in both understanding and treating psychopathologies.

Considering emotions in psychopathology; emotional dysregulation, intensity, and lability contribute to conditions such as bipolar disorder, borderline personality disorder, and anxiety disorders.

Accordingly, the inability to regulate emotional responses can contribute to severe mood swings in bipolar disorder or inappropriate anger in borderline personality disorder (D'Aurizo et al., 2023). Emotion plays a significant role in psychopathology.

Further examining emotions in mental illness; emotional dysregulation, observed in conditions such as anxiety, depression, and borderline personality disorder, is defined by overwhelming and uncontrollable emotions. The dysregulation can lead to challenges in everyday activities and interpersonal connections (Millgram et al., 2020). In addition, individuals struggling with emotion dysregulation may experience heightened emotional reactivity, impulsivity, and difficulty in effectively modulating their emotional responses (Millgram et al., 2020). Emotions can also influence cognition, with emotional states shaping how individuals understand and perceive the environment.

Emotion intensity in psychopathology refers to the extreme and overwhelming nature of emotional experiences that individuals may face. This can manifest as highly intense emotional reactions to various situations, stimuli, or triggers, often disproportionate to the actual event (Millgram et al., 2020). Research showed the relationship between intense emotional states and various mental illnesses such as bipolar, anxiety, and borderline personality disorders (Millgram et al., 2020). The intensity of emotions in these conditions can lead to challenges in regulating and maintaining emotional stability, underscoring the importance of understanding and addressing emotion dysregulation in mental health treatment. Experiencing heightened emotion intensity can impact daily functioning, relationships, and overall mental well-being.

Moreover, emotional lability is defined by rapid and intense shifts in emotions, resulting in individuals swiftly transitioning between different emotional states. Those with emotional lability often struggle to control their emotions, resulting in exaggerated reactions to emotional stimuli. Moreover, emotion lability can impact various aspects of daily functioning and relationships, as individuals may struggle to maintain emotional stability and predictability in their reactions (Leaberry et al., 2020). Effective management of emotion lability often involves therapy and strategies focused on emotion regulation and coping skills.

Motivation is another key aspect of psychopathology. In psychopathology, motivation is often characterized by a lack or excess of motivation, as seen in disorders like depression (reduced motivation) or mania (excessive motivation). Anhedonia, or the loss of interest in pleasurable activities, is a significant motivational symptom in depression (Steinmann et al., 2022). Additionally, insights into motivational issues have led to motivational interviewing and other techniques designed to enhance motivation for behavioral change, especially in addiction and depression (Bischof et al., 2021). Moreover, individuals with certain disorders, such as substance use disorders, may experience disruptions in motivation, leading to difficulties in maintaining relationships, employment, and overall functioning (Bischof et al., 2021). Motivation can also influence treatment outcomes, as individuals with low motivation may be less likely to engage in therapeutic interventions and make positive changes in their lives.

In summary, research findings in the field of psychology are significant for acquiring knowledge of the underlying mechanisms of psychopathology and developing effective interventions. Studies on cognition have led to the development of widely used cognitive based therapies and treatments. Research on emotion regulation has informed interventions aimed at helping individuals better manage their emotions and reduce symptoms of psychopathology. Additionally, research on motivation has led to the development of motivational interviewing techniques, which are effective in promoting behavior change.

## Factors and Influences

Different personal, environmental, and sociocultural factors, influences, and components contribute to the development of cognition, emotion, and motivation in psychopathology. For example, genetic predispositions, personality traits, early life experiences, and social support all can contribute to an individual's vulnerabilities to psychopathologies (Smith et al., 2020).

Personal characteristics have a significant impact on the formation of psychopathology.

Personal factors can include genetic and biological predispositions, as well as individual differences in personality and cognitive functioning. Studies have demonstrated that specific genetic traits can elevate a person's likelihood of developing conditions like depression or schizophrenia (Alshaya, 2022). Additionally, personality traits such as neuroticism or impulsivity are in some instances related to an enhanced vulnerability to psychopathology. For example, the diathesis-stress model illustrates how personal vulnerabilities interact with life stresses to trigger disorders.

Accordingly, a theoretical concept in psychopathology, (diathesis-stress model), offers insight into how conditions stem from a consort of genetic predispositions and susceptibilities and environmental stressors. It posits that those with a genetic or biological susceptibility may be more prone to developing a disorder when faced with challenging life circumstances (stressors). (Salomon & Jin, 2020). Overall, the model highlights the interplay between nature (genetics) and nurture (environment) in the development of psychopathology.

Additionally genetic and biological factors, along with variations in personality and cognitive abilities, are crucial factors in the progression of psychopathology. Studies have indicated that specific genetic variables can elevate the likelihood of conditions like depression or schizophrenia in individuals (Alshaya, 2022). Also, traits like neuroticism and impulsivity have been associated with heightened susceptibility to mental health disorders.

Moreover, certain personality traits, like neuroticism and extraversion, can increase the likelihood of psychopathology. Particularly, individuals with high neuroticism can be more susceptible to disorders such as anxiety or mood disorders. (Regzedmaa et al., 2024). Also, individuals low in extraversion may possibly experience social isolation and lonesomeness (Stavrova, 2021). Further, research has also highlighted the role of early life experiences, such as attachment style or childhood trauma, in shaping cognitive and emotional processes that can contribute to the development of psychopathology.

Subsequently, research has identified specific mental disorders linked to different gene groups within families and ethnicities. However, individuals with the same disorder can display varied symptoms (Forbes et al., 2021). The genetic and neurological systems that add and delete neurons from the brain has a substantial part in the manifestation of mental illness (Alshaya, 2022). Genes seem to play a role in the onset of mental illnesses in three main ways: they can dictate the underlying causes of disorders like Alzheimer's and schizophrenia, lead to developmental issues in individuals before or after birth, and impact an individual's predisposition towards conditions like anxiety, depression, personality disorders, and substance abuse disorders (Alshaya, 2022). Further, practitioners have become increasingly informed of the significance of hereditary variables in the pathogenesis of psychopathology.

Nonetheless, environmental factors can have a significant impact on the emergence of mental disorders. These factors can include early life experiences, trauma, and stressors such as poverty or discrimination (Williams et al., 2019). Research has shown that individuals who experience childhood trauma or adverse life events are at an increased risk for development of disorders across the life span (Kalin, 2020). Furthermore, research has shown that chronic stress can have a detrimental impact on the brain and increase the risk of developing mental health problems (Hopwood et al., 2022). This underscores the significance of reducing environmental stressors in the management of psychopathology. Additionally, social support and access to resources can act as protective factors against the development of psychopathology.

Sociocultural components are also important to consider when studying psychopathology. These factors can include cultural norms, societal expectations, and stigmas surrounding mental health (Scerri et al., 2019). Studies have demonstrated that certain cultural beliefs or attitudes towards mental illness can impact an individual's willingness to seek help or access treatment (Williams et al., 2019). Additionally, psychopathology can stem from societal pressures or discrimination.

Further in terms of sociocultural components, research has delved deeper into the sociocultural aspects by exploring differences in how mental disorders are expressed across different cultures. For example, individuals from collectivistic cultures may be more likely to somaticize psychological distress, leading to physical symptoms rather than emotional ones (Goodmann et al., 2021). Understanding these cultural nuances is crucial in providing culturally sensitive and effective treatment for individuals with psychopathology.

In summarizing, within psychopathology, personal features encompass genetic propensities, personality traits, and cognitive functioning, where genetic and biological vulnerabilities can interact with stressful life events, as proposed by the diathesis-stress model. Environmental influences, such as early life experiences and chronic stress, can also significantly impact the development of mental health issues (Kalin, 2020). Sociocultural components, including cultural norms and societal expectations, further contribute to the complexity of psychopathology by influencing help-seeking behaviors and perceptions of mental health. Practitioners recognize the significance of addressing both genetics and environmental features when identifying and treating psychopathology effectively.

## Integrating Factors

Key determinants in shaping the cognitive, emotional, and motivational aspects that contribute to psychopathology encompass personal factors, environmental influences, and sociocultural components. For example, personal characteristics like genetic makeup, inherent personality traits, and life experiences all contribute to influencing how an individual reacts mentally and emotionally to stressful situations (Joormam, 2019). Moreover, individual differences in traits or coping strategies can impact cognition, emotion, and motivation. Individuals who tend to ruminate or engage in negative self-talk may be more susceptible to developing depressive symptoms (Ehring, 2021). Also, personal experiences, such as trauma or abuse, can impact emotional well-being and motivation.

Environmental influences, including family dynamics, social support, and traumatic events, can impact how these factors manifest in behavior (Hopwood et al., 2022). Sociocultural factors like societal expectations, cultural values, and financial condition can impact how individuals experience psychopathology and affect their willingness to seek assistance or receive treatment. Additionally, sociocultural factors can influence cognition, emotion, and motivation is through societal norms and expectations. For example, individuals may internalize societal beliefs or attitudes that dictate how they should think, feel, or behave, leading to cognitive distortions and maladaptive emotional responses (Scerri et al., 2021). Differences in cultural customs and beliefs can influence how an individual interprets and displays their feelings, potentially affecting their well-being. The integration of these factors can create complex interactions that can either exacerbate or ameliorate symptoms of psychopathology, highlighting the importance of a holistic approach to understanding and addressing mental health challenges.

In summary, the exploration of cognition, emotion, and motivation within the context of psychopathology provides a comprehensive understanding of how psychological disorders develop, manifest, and can be treated. These elements are interconnected with personal factors, environmental influences, and sociocultural components, each contributing to the complexity of mental health issues. In psychopathology, cognitive, emotional, and motivational factors can be influenced in various ways. For example, individuals with certain disorders may experience distorted thinking patterns that affect their cognitive processing, heightened emotional responses that impact their mood regulation, and altered motivational goals that guide their behavior. Additionally, the interplay between these factors can further exacerbate symptoms and support manifestation of psychopathology. Understanding these interactions is critical for developing effective interventions and treatments for individuals experiencing mental health challenges.

Overall, integrating cognition processes, emotional states, and motivational factors with personal, environmental, and sociocultural factors provides a more holistic view of psychopathology. This integrated approach not only improves our understanding of mental health disorders but also enhances the efficacy of interventions and supports the development of preventative measures, significantly impacting the broader field of psychology.

## Neuropsychology and Psychopathology

Research in neuropsychology has provided valuable insights into understanding psychopathology, including schizophrenia, major depressive disorders, and personality disorders. Neuropsychology's focus is how the brain and nervous system affect behavior (Gkintoni, 2023). The discipline explores various psychopathological conditions by using clinical neuroscience to investigate the cognitive and neurobiological underpinnings of behavior associated with conditions.

One recent study in neuropsychology examined the relationship between brain structure and antisocial behavior. The researchers found that individuals who displayed violent and aggressive behavior had differences in the structure of their prefrontal cortex, according to the researchers, there were variations in the prefrontal cortex structure of people exhibiting violent and aggressive behaviors, highlighting the significance of cognitive functions in regulating impulsivity and making decisions (Friedman & Robbins, 2022). Teleanu et al. (2022) explored the role of neurotransmitters, such as serotonin and dopamine, in the development of psychopathology. The researchers found that imbalances in these neurotransmitters can contribute to the onset and severity of symptoms, underscoring the impact of emotions on mental well-being.

Additionally, recent research in neuropsychology has examined how trauma experienced in childhood impacts brain development and brain maturation and influences the chances of developing disorders in the future. A neuropsychological study revealed that individuals who underwent childhood abuse displayed changes in brain structure and function, increasing their susceptibility to conditions like PTSD and depression (Ibrahim et al., 2021). These findings can highlight factors interacting in psychopathology within the context of neuropsychology. Further, current research in neuropsychology continues to provide valuable insights into the underlying mechanisms of psychopathology and potential avenues for treatment and intervention.

## Significance

Research findings on psychopathology are vital in clinical practice and the overall field of psychology for comprehending the causes, symptoms, and treatments for psychological issues. Studies on cognition have led to the development of cognitive-behavioral therapy, research on emotion regulation has informed interventions to better manage emotions, and research on motivation has led to effective behavior change techniques. By considering various factors and promoting awareness about mental health, these findings help in identification, prevention, and tailored interventions for individuals with psychopathology, ultimately improving mental health outcomes and reducing stigma.

Further, through examining the relationship between individual, environmental, and sociocultural elements, researchers can use the results in clinical settings to recognize potential triggers for mental illnesses, create methods for prevention, and customize treatments to address the unique requirements of individuals grappling with psychopathology. Additionally, research helps to destigmatize mental illness and promote awareness and acceptance of individuals struggling with mental health issues (Scerri et al., 2019). Overall, research findings in the field of psychology are critical for bettering the quality of life of individuals living through psychopathology and advancing the field of mental health.

***Thanks!***

## References


Alshaya, D. S. (2022). Genetic and epigenetic factors associated with depression: An updated overview. *Saudi Journal of Biological Sciences*, *29*(8). https://doi.org/10.1016/j.sjbs.2022.103311

Bischof, G., Bischof, A., & Rumpf, H. J. (2021). Motivational interviewing: an evidence-based approach for use in medical practice. *Deutsches Ärzteblatt International*, *118*(7), 109. https://doi.org/10.3238/arztebl.m2021.0014

D'Aurizio, G., Di Stefano, R., Socci, V., Rossi, A., Barlattani, T., Pacitti, F., & Rossi, R. (2023). The role of emotional instability in borderline personality disorder: A systematic review. *Annals of General Psychiatry, 22*(1). https://doi.org/10.1186/s12991-023-00439-0

Ehring, T. (2021). Thinking too much: Rumination and psychopathology. *World Psychiatry*, *20*(3), 441. https://doi.org/10.1002/wps.20910

Forbes, M. K., Sunderland, M., Rapee, R. M., Batterham, P. J., Calear, A. L., Carragher, N., & Krueger, R. F. (2021). A detailed hierarchical model of psychopathology: From individual symptoms up to the general factor of psychopathology. *Clinical Psychological Science*, *9*(2), 139-168. https://doi.org/10.1177/2167702620954799

Friedman, N. P., & Robbins, T. W. (2022). The role of prefrontal cortex in cognitive control and executive function. *Neuropsychopharmacology*, *47*(1), 72-89. https://doi.org/10.1038/s41386-021-01132-0

Gkintoni, E. (2023). Clinical neuropsychological characteristics of bipolar disorder, with a focus on cognitive and linguistic pattern: A conceptual analysis. *F1000Research*, 12, 1235. https://doi.org/10.12688/f1000research.141599.1

Goodmann, D. R., Daouk, S., Sullivan, M., Cabrera, J., Liu, N. H., Barakat, S., Muñoz, R. F., & Leykin, Y. (2021). Factor analysis of depression symptoms across five broad cultural groups. *Journal of Affective Disorders*, 282, 227–235. https://doi.org/10.1016/j.jad.2020.12.159

Hopwood, C. J., Wright, A. G., & Bleidorn, W. (2022). Person–environment transactions differentiate personality and psychopathology. *Nature Reviews Psychology*, *1*(1), 55-63. https://doi.org/10.1038/s44159-021-00004-0

Jiang, Y. (2024). A theory of the neural mechanisms underlying negative cognitive bias in major depression. *Frontiers in Psychiatry*, 15. https://doi.org/10.3389/fpsyt.2024.1348474

Joormann, J. (2019). Is the glass half empty or half full and does it even matter? Cognition, emotion, and psychopathology. *Cognition and Emotion, 33*(1), 133–138. https://doi.org/10.1080/02699931.2018.1502656

Kalin, N. H. (2020). Early-life environmental factors impacting the development of psychopathology. *American Journal of Psychiatry*, *177*(1), 1-3. https://doi.org/10.1176/appi.ajp.2019.19111181

Kube, T., Schwarting, R., Rozenkrantz, L., Glombiewski, J. A., & Rief, W. (2020). Distorted cognitive processes in major depression: A predictive processing perspective. *Biological Psychiatry, 87*(5), 388-398. https://doi.org/10.1016/j.biopsych.2019.07.017

Leaberry, K. D., Walerius, D. M., Rosen, P. J., & Fogleman, N. D. (2020). Emotional lability. *Encyclopedia of personality and individual differences*, 1319-1329. https://doi.org/10.1007/978-3-319-24612-3_510

Millgram, Y., Huppert, J. D., & Tamir, M. (2020). Emotion goals in psychopathology: A new perspective on dysfunctional emotion regulation. *Current Directions in Psychological Science*, *29*(3), 242-247. https://doi.org/10.1177/0963721420917713

Regzedmaa, E., Ganbat, M., Sambuunyam, M., Tsogoo, S., Radnaa, O., Lkhagvasuren, N., & Zuunnast, K. (2024). A systematic review and meta-analysis of neuroticism and anxiety during the COVID-19 pandemic. *Frontiers in Psychiatry*, 14. https://doi.org/10.3389/fpsyt.2023.1281268

Salomon, K., & Jin, A. (2020). Diathesis-stress model. In *Encyclopedia of behavioral medicine* (pp. 655-657). Cham: Springer International Publishing. https://doi.org/10.1007/978-3-030-39903-0_797

Scerri, J., Sammut, A., & Agius, J. (2023). A sociocultural perspective of mental health stigma in Malta. *Frontiers in Psychiatry*, 14. https://doi.org/10.3389/fpsyt.2023.1229920

Smith, G. T., Atkinson, E. A., Davis, H. A., Riley, E. N., & Oltmanns, J. R. (2020). The general factor of psychopathology. *Annual Review of Clinical Psychology*, *16*, 75-98. https://doi.org/10.1146/annurev-clinpsy-071119-115848

Stavrova, O., Ren, D., & Pronk, T. (2022). Low self-control: a hidden cause of loneliness?. *Personality and Social Psychology Bulletin, 48*(3), 347-362. https://doi: 10.1177/01461672211007228

Steinmann, L. A., Dohm, K., Goltermann, J., Richter, M., Enneking, V., Lippitz, M., Repple, J., Mauritz, M., Dannlowski, U., & Opel, N. (2022). Understanding the neurobiological basis of anhedonia in major depressive disorder - evidence for reduced neural activation during reward and loss processing. *Journal of Psychiatry and Neuroscience, 47*(4). E284–E292. https://doi.org/10.1503/jpn.210180

Teleanu, R. I., Niculescu, A. G., Roza, E., Vladâcenco, O., Grumezescu, A. M., & Teleanu, D. M. (2022). Neurotransmitters - key factors in neurological and neurodegenerative disorders of the central nervous system. *International Journal of Molecular Sciences, 23*(11), 5954. https://doi.org/10.3390/ijms23115954

Williams, D. R., Lawrence, J. A., Davis, B. A., & Vu, C. (2019). Understanding how discrimination can affect health. *Health Services Research, 54*(S2), 1374–1388. Portico. https://doi.org/10.1111/1475-6773.13222

www.ingramcontent.com/pod-product-compliance
Lightning Source LLC
Chambersburg PA
CBHW051405250726
48656CB00006B/2282